W9-AYE-083

American
JAZZ
MILES
DAVIS

TAMRA ORR

Mitchell Lane
PUBLISHERS

P.O. Box 196
Hockessin, Delaware 19707

American JAZZ

Benny Goodman

Bessie Smith

Billie Holiday

Charlie Parker

Count Basie

Dizzy Gillespie

Louis Armstrong

Miles Davis

Ornette Coleman

Scott Joplin

PUBLISHER'S NOTE: The facts on which this book is based have been thoroughly researched. Documentation of such research can be found on page 44. While every possible effort has been made to ensure accuracy, the publisher will not assume liability for damages caused by inaccuracies in the data, and makes no warranty on the accuracy of the information contained herein.

Printing   1   2   3   4   5   6   7   8   9

Library of Congress Cataloging-in-Publication Data

Orr, Tamra.
  Miles Davis / by Tamra Orr.
    pages ; cm. — (American jazz)
  Includes bibliographical references and index.
  ISBN 978-1-61228-265-7 (library bound)
  1. Davis, Miles—Juvenile literature. 2. Jazz musicians—United States—Juvenile literature.
  I. Title.
  ML3930.D33O77 2013
  788.9'2165092—dc23
  [B]
                     2012008632

eBook ISBN: 9781612283418

                   PLB

Contents

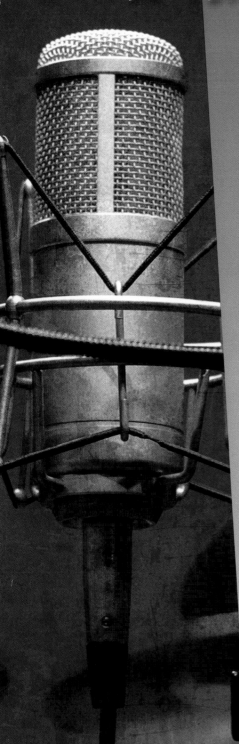

Chapter **1**

Weathering an Argument

It was Miles's thirteenth birthday. What would his present be? he wondered. He knew what he really wanted, but he was not sure that his parents would ever be able to agree on it. In fact, he could hear his parents fighting about it in the other room.

Arguing was not uncommon in the Davis household. Miles Dewey Davis Jr., Miles's father, and Cleota Mae Henry Davis, his mother, were known for not getting along. Years later, those disagreements would lead to a divorce. Although the two of them loved each other and were raising three children together, they quarreled often about what was best for their two sons and daughter. Little Miles's birthday was no exception.

Both of Miles's parents agreed that their son loved music and that it would most likely play a large role in his life. After all, since he was seven years old, he had been listening to a radio show called *Harlem Rhythms*. The show featured some of the hottest black musicians of the time, such as Louis Armstrong, Count Basie, and Duke Ellington. "The show used to come on at fifteen minutes to nine every day, so I was late to school a lot because I was listening to that program," Davis wrote in his autobiography. "But I *had* to hear that show, man, had to."[1]

When Miles was not quite ten years old, one of his father's friends, Dr. John Eubanks, gave the young boy a trumpet. He loved it! He even took some private music lessons so he could learn how to play a few simple songs. He knew he had found his passion. He and his brother and sister would hold talent shows together. While Dorothy played the piano or acted out some skits she wrote, Miles played his trumpet and little Vernon danced. Miles knew what he wanted to do with his life. In his autobiography he wrote, "When I got into music, I went all the way into music; I didn't have no time after that for nothing else."[2]

Just the Right Gift

Now that his birthday was here, Miles's parents wanted to get him a better instrument—but what kind to get spurred a family argument. Cleota wanted her son to pursue a career in what she called "serious music," which meant classical. To her, this style of music represented being cultured and being accepted into the white community. She had played the violin when she was younger, and that's what she thought young Miles should have for his thirteenth birthday.

Dr. Davis had other ideas. He hoped that his son would become a dentist like he was, or at least get a degree in some type of medical profession; but he also recognized his son's fascination for music—just not classical. He knew that his young son was much more interested in the new swinging music being played in the clubs and streets of the city than he was in classical scores. It was known as jazz, and it all centered on brass instruments and pianos. The wail of shiny trumpets, cornets, and trombones was the focus of most jazz bands, giving them life and energy. Young Miles was particularly interested in the trumpet, and the few lessons he had had so far were not enough. He wanted more!

Dr. Davis wanted his son to have a new trumpet—and had, in fact, already bought him one, even though Cleota was furious with him for it. "My mother wanted me to have a violin, but my father overruled her," Davis recalled in his autobiography. "This caused a big argument between them."[3] The trumpet disagreement became just another wedge between them before the two eventually split completely.

So What solo

Miles Davis

The birthday gift was not simply the trumpet. Dr. Davis had also arranged for his son to take lessons with a local jazz musician and teacher named Elwood Buchanan. Dr. Davis had met Buchanan at work and the two had become friends. He had arranged to have Buchanan teach his son. Later, in his autobiography, Miles wrote that Buchanan became one of the biggest influences in his life. "He was definitely the person who took me all the way into music at that time," he wrote.[4]

Getting a real trumpet—and lessons for how to play it—was a turning point for the teenage Miles Davis. Until this time, he had had many different interests, including sports. He was a great runner and was fascinated by boxing. He had even thought about finding a career as an athlete. These trumpet lessons changed his mind. "I knew I wanted to become a musician. That was all I wanted to be," he later wrote.[5]

Although Miles Davis ended up pursuing a career in music, his fascination with sports, including boxing, stayed with him throughout his life.

By the time he was in high school, Miles was taking the first steps toward becoming one of the biggest and most memorable jazz performers in the world. Not even Elwood Buchanan knew that the young man he was teaching would eventually be known everywhere as one of the most talented and inventive trumpeters in the world.

The World of Jazz

Davis could not have picked a better time to explore the world of jazz. The Great Depression was finally over, and the country was looking to the future with hope. This excitement was reflected in a growing appreciation of music. People were spending money on records again. Business owners were adding jukeboxes to their restaurants. Hollywood was hiring actors who could sing and dance for the musicals the filmmakers planned to produce.

In the clubs, bandleaders like Benny Goodman were creating the Swing Era, featuring songs with complicated arrangements. The audiences loved them, and by the mid-1940s, Goodman, Cole Porter, and other musicians were selling millions of records. Songwriters such as George Gershwin and Irving Berlin were providing tunes that developed into some of the best jazz standards in history.

Once the 1940s began, swing was still popular, but it slowly gave way to a new style known as bebop. Even though another world war had begun, audiences still enjoyed jazz bands for exciting tunes that were fun to dance to. Songs like "In the Mood" and "Tuxedo Junction" were playing on most radio stations, and even the movies included jazz tunes like "Chattanooga Choo Choo." This ever-changing world of jazz was just right for Davis to explore and discover.

Chapter **2**

Getting an Early Start

Unlike many of his future fellow musicians, Miles Dewey Davis III did not have a difficult or poor start in life. Instead, he was born on May 25, 1926, to a mother who was a music teacher and a father who was a successful dentist, with three separate college degrees. The family had a nice home in Alton, Illinois, as well as a 200-acre estate out in the country, where Miles and siblings Dorothy and Vernon grew up riding horses, fishing, and hunting.

At Crispus Attucks School, Davis was a good student, excelling in math, music, and sports. He was small and shy, however, and was often called "Little Davis." Learning to master the trumpet helped him become more confident. "I was a small, skinny kid with the skinniest legs anybody ever had," he wrote in his autobiography. "But I loved sports so much, I couldn't be intimidated or scared by people bigger than me."[1]

By the time he was fifteen years old, Davis was playing in Lincoln High School's marching band. He spent hours practicing his trumpet every day and entered every possible music competition he could. In later writings he stated that the contests he did not win were largely due to prejudice against his race. At the same time, he credits that prejudice with driving him to become a better musician.

Miles Davis (left) was fortunate enough to grow up in a relatively wealthy family, along with his sister Dorothy Mae, his brother Vernon, and his mother Cleota.

Getting Offers

Although Davis was still a teenager, his ability on the trumpet was slowly becoming known among local jazz players. He would ride across the river to St. Louis, Missouri, to listen to jazz performers in clubs playing bebop songs. In 1943, thanks to Buchanan's recommendation, Davis tried out for a part in the local favorite jazz band, Eddie Randle's Blue Devils. He got it and soon was performing with them at nearby clubs. Later he also joined the Billy Eckstine Band. During his performances, he often had the chance to meet some of the biggest names in jazz, including Dizzy Gillespie and his future idol, Charlie "Yardbird" Parker.

When Davis was offered a job with a touring band, he was thrilled—but Cleota was not. "I went home and asked my mother if I could go

Davis (back row, right) learned a great deal about performing during his time with Eddie Randle's Rhumboogie Orchestra, also known as the Blue Devils. His parents were not thrilled with their son's choice of profession, however.

with them," he recalled years later in an interview with *DownBeat* magazine. "She said no, I had to finish my last year of high school. I didn't talk to her for two weeks. And I didn't go with the band either."[2]

After Davis graduated in 1944, it was little surprise that his parents could not agree on what their son should do next. Cleota wanted Davis to go to Fisk University in Nashville, Tennessee. Dorothy was already enrolled there. The college had an excellent music department, and Cleota still had hopes her son would take up either the violin or the piano.

Dr. Davis knew better. He knew that his son had set his sights on going to New York City's Juilliard School of Music, then known as the

Institute of Musical Arts. Once again, Dr. Davis won the argument, and in the fall of 1944, Miles enrolled in Juilliard. That same year, his parents finally divorced, and Miles became a father for the first time. He and his girlfriend, Irene Birth, had a daughter they named Cheryl.

Making a Choice

Although Juilliard was a wonderful school, Davis was not happy there. The music he studied was not his style. He wanted to be on stage, under the spotlight, playing alongside Charlie Parker, Dizzy Gillespie, and the other musicians who filled the clubs on New York's 52nd Street—known as Swing Street—with energy and excitement. Sitting in class studying classical music may have been what his mother wanted, but it was not what Davis wanted. Instead, he wanted to learn from the mentors he was listening to every night. They were willing to teach him, too. Davis wrote, "Every night I'd write down chords I heard on matchbook covers. Everybody helped me. Next day I'd play those chords all day in the practice room at Juilliard instead of going to classes."[3]

Finally, after the summer semester of 1945, Davis had had enough. He quit Juilliard so that he could play full-time in the local clubs. "I told my father to save his money," he recalled in an interview with *Esquire* magazine. His father accepted Miles's decision and even had some advice for his determined son. According to Davis's autobiography, Dr. Davis said, " 'Miles, you hear that bird outside the window? He's a mockingbird. He don't have a sound of his own. He copies everybody's sound, and you don't want to do that. . . . So, don't be nobody else but yourself. You know what you got to do and I trust your judgment.' "[4] Then he promised that he would keep sending Miles money until he could earn enough on his own.

Leaving Juilliard to play for Parker's band full-time was a scary decision, but it was one that Miles never regretted. "I was playing with the greatest jazz musicians in the world, so what did I have to feel bad about?" he wrote in his autobiography. "Nothing. And I didn't. Never looked back."[5] Davis was on his way to fame and fortune, horn in hand.

Charlie "Yardbird" Parker

Like his protégé, Charlie Parker began playing jazz music when he was just a teenager. When he was in junior high, he joined the school band, playing the baritone horn. By the time he was sixteen years old, he was already married and playing the alto saxophone in a band. He and a few other jazz musicians were responsible for creating a different kind of music known as bebop.

Parker played in a number of bands and clubs in jazz hubs like Kansas City, Missouri; Chicago; and New York City. By 1945, he had his own band, and together they went on a tour of Hollywood nightclubs.

By the time he met young Miles Davis, Parker—or Yardbird, or just Bird, as he was called—had struggled with an addiction to drugs and alcohol. He had even spent some time in a state mental institution after having a nervous breakdown. Despite all this, Parker was able to make a strong comeback and even had a nightclub in New York named after him.

Charlie Parker and Miles Davis

Birdland was one of the most famous clubs in the country during the 1950s and was written about in songs. In the late 1940s and early 1950s, Parker toured Europe and recorded a number of albums. Sadly, years of alcohol abuse caught up with him in 1955, and at only thirty-four years old, he died of a heart attack.

Chapter 3

Breaking an Addiction

Although Miles Davis's talent and skill on the trumpet kept climbing, his life was not necessarily an easy one. Already the father to one child with his girlfriend Irene, he soon had a second child with her. This time it was a son named Gregory, born in 1946. A year later, Irene and her children moved to New York to be with Davis. In 1950, she had another baby, Miles Davis IV.

Davis kept working on his music, slowly shifting from bebop to a richer, more unique sound called cool jazz. The clubs on 52nd Street gave way to higher-class clubs near the Broadway region. Sometimes he played solo; other times he performed with one or two other players and sometimes with a full band. He formed a nine-piece band, called the Miles Davis Nonet, and began working with arranger Gil Evans. The group was made of Davis on the trumpet, plus others playing a trombone, tuba, French horn, baritone saxophone, alto saxophone, piano, bass, and drums. Now and then a singer joined the group. Who was in the band seemed to change often, but Davis's band worked together for more than twenty years.

In 1949 and 1950, in three different sessions, the Miles Davis Nonet recorded a dozen songs. The resulting album was called *Birth of the Cool*, and although it was not released for several years, it is still thought of as one of Davis's best performances.

The Miles Davis Nonet gathered at Capitol Records to record *Birth of the Cool*. Sixty years later, this album would still be considered one of the best examples of jazz music ever produced.

An Addictive Time

As Davis searched for the right sound and music, he also struggled with trying to be a family man—a job that he did not like and which was often at odds with his music career. Being a husband and father was not what he had in mind. His focus was his music.

To complicate matters, like many of the other musicians with whom he performed, Davis had developed an addiction to heroin, a powerful and dangerous drug. He also drank large amounts of alcohol and frequently used cocaine. All of this took a toll on his mental and physical health. It also made it harder to concentrate on his music, because he spent so much time looking for drugs, using them, recovering from them, and then starting all over again. In his autobiography, Davis wrote about how the drugs affected his life: "I turned into one of the best hustlers because I had to get heroin every day, no matter what I had to do."[1] This included stealing from his friends and pawning his horn to get more money. At one point he was even arrested for possessing drugs. It became harder and harder for him to find jobs because club managers were frightened of hiring someone as unreliable as Davis was proving to be.

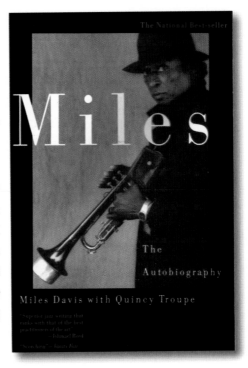

Time for Change

The constant drug use was ruining Davis's life. He was no longer with Irene or his children, and it was getting harder and harder to hold down any music job. Finally, in 1953, Davis turned to the person who always seemed to be there for him: his father. He asked Dr. Davis for enough money to ride the bus out to their estate in the country. Dr. Davis was honest with his son once he arrived. "I can't do nothing for you, son, but give you my love and support. The rest of it you got to do for yourself."[2] Then he walked away.

For the next two weeks, Davis stayed locked up inside a small apartment on the estate. It wasn't easy—in fact, it was one of the most difficult experiences of his life. "You feel like you could die and if somebody could guarantee that you would die in two seconds, then you would take it," he wrote. Finally, the pain of withdrawal was over. "I walked outside into the clean, sweet air over to my father's house, and when he saw me, he had this big smile on his face and we just hugged each other and cried," he wrote. "Then I sat down and started thinking about how I was going to get my life back together, which wasn't going to be an easy task."[3]

Davis's time at his father's had helped—but it was not a final solution. When the musician moved to Detroit to start playing again, old habits kicked in, and he was soon using drugs once more. This time it was his fascination with African-American boxer Sugar Ray Robinson that inspired him. "Sugar Ray was the hero-image that I carried in my mind," he recalled. "It was him that made me think that I was strong enough to deal with New York City again. And it was his example that pulled me through some real tough days."[4]

This time, Davis locked himself into a Detroit, Michigan, hotel room for twelve days. When he emerged, his addiction was over—and he never went back to it.

Sugar Ray Robinson

A Life-Changing Performance

Most of the jazz fans who had spent time in big cities such as Chicago, Detroit, Los Angeles, or New York knew of Miles Davis and his ability to blow a trumpet like no other. They had heard him find his own style, as he played alone and with groups of four, six, or nine. It was the summer of 1955, however, that brought Miles Davis to the attention of jazz fans all over the country.

In Rhode Island, the second annual Newport Jazz Festival was being held. Miles Davis was added to the list of performers at the last minute. He took the stage along with several other well-known jazz musicians,

The Newport Jazz Festival began in 1954 and was attracting thousands of music fans each year more than half a century later. Davis performed at the festival in 1955 and 1969, with Jack DeJohnette on drums and Dave Holland on bass. Besides Davis, this three-day festival has featured jazz icons such as Louis Armstrong, Duke Ellington, and Ella Fitzgerald.

Thelonious Monk was born in 1917. By the time he was thirteen years old, he had won Apollo Theater's amateur talent contest so many times, he was not allowed to enter any more. As one of the biggest creators of the bebop sound, he was both a talented pianist as well as a composer. He wrote many songs that went on to become jazz classics, including " 'Round Midnight." The Thelonious Monk Institute of Jazz was established to honor his contribution to jazz.

including Thelonious Monk, and blew several solos on songs that included " 'Round Midnight." When he was finished, the crowd went wild. They loved his style and wanted to hear more.

Reporters began interviewing Davis, and it was not long before he had a recording contract with Columbia Records. To perform, he put together some of his favorite players, creating a quintet with Red Garland (piano), Philly Joe Jones (drums), Paul Chambers (bass), and John Coltrane (saxophone). Later, he added a sixth player, saxophonist Cannonball Adderly. Together, the sextet produced some of the best jazz albums in the world—including one that would beat all previous and current records. There was no doubt that Miles Davis was back—and going strong!

Although Miles Davis was becoming a star on the stage, when he stepped off it, he faced the same prejudice shared by other African Americans. The 1950s were a time of huge transition for the civil rights movement. In 1954, the Supreme Court case *Brown v. Board of Education* ruled that blacks had the right to attend all public schools. Even though the ruling was in place, it took years before African-American children could actually walk through the front doors of integrated schools without threats and harassment. In 1955, a yearlong boycott of the public bus system began as blacks fought for the right to take any seat in the vehicles. The movement was led by activists Rosa Parks and Martin Luther King Jr. Their determination inspired other racial equality leaders across the country and motivated events such as lunch counter sit-ins and other nonviolent protests.

Davis had to face prejudice and discrimination multiple times during his career. He once told television interviewer Dick Cavett that he had gotten tired of being stopped by the police whenever he drove his fancy red Ferrari. Davis stated that when the police saw a black man driving an expensive car, they assumed he had stolen it. He had been pulled over repeatedly and asked if he were the rightful owner of the car. Finally, Davis had had enough and obtained a license plate that stated, "SHE'S MINE."

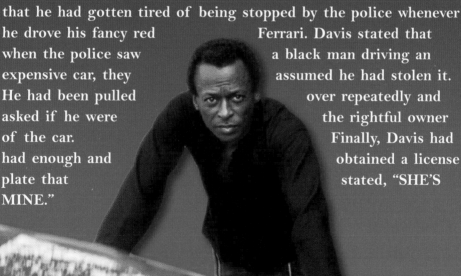

Chapter 4

Hitting the Charts—and Getting Hit

The next two decades certainly must have felt like a roller coaster for Miles Davis. He hit all-new highs, but he also discovered some new lows. Now that he was free of the damages of drug addiction, he was able to focus more on his music. Although clean of serious drugs like cocaine and heroin, he was still drinking alcohol heavily and abusing less dangerous drugs. It was certainly taking a toll on his health. He was often exhausted and stressed, giving in to bouts of anger. During the 1950s, he produced a huge variety of albums, including *Miles Ahead*, *Milestones*, and *Kind of Blue*. This third album, released in 1959, has sold more than four million copies since then, and is considered the bestselling jazz record in history.

Despite his success in the music world, Davis still struggled personally. In 1957, he had surgery to remove nodes on his vocal cords. While he was still recovering and was to stay quiet, he yelled at someone and damaged his throat permanently. Two years later, while standing on a sidewalk in New York, a police officer asked him to "move along." When Davis refused, a second police officer began hitting the musician over the head with a baton, and then hauled him off to jail for the night. Davis's wound needed five stitches, and the incident was splashed all over the newspapers, radio, and television. It took almost a year for the city of New York to drop the charges against

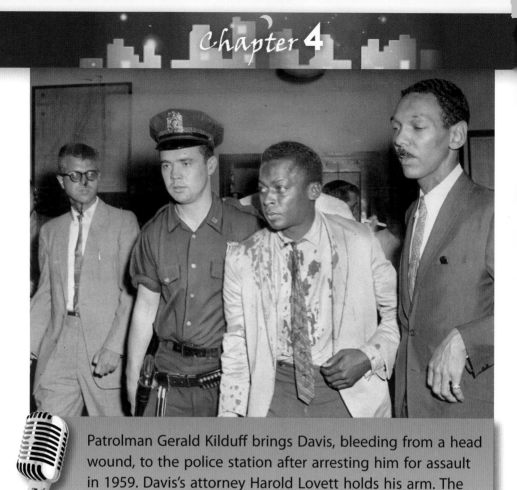

Patrolman Gerald Kilduff brings Davis, bleeding from a head wound, to the police station after arresting him for assault in 1959. Davis's attorney Harold Lovett holds his arm. The arrest led to a great deal of controversy about racial prejudice and civil rights.

Davis. Whether it occurred because he had been drinking and behaving badly or because he simply was outside taking a break in between numbers is still debated. Either way, this incident only made Davis angrier and more bitter.

Success—and Frustration

By 1961, Miles Davis was the highest paid and best-known jazz musician in the world. He was performing in front of sold-out crowds throughout the United States and Europe. His struggle to find a woman with whom he could be happy—and who could be happy with him in return—continued. He had been married to a dancer named Frances Taylor, but the marriage lasted only a few years. Next he married Betty Mabry, a much younger woman, and they did not reach a year together before divorcing. In 1970, his fourth child, son Erin, was born.

At the same time, Davis found himself frustrated with his music. Although he had produced a popular album called *Quiet Nights,* he was not happy with it. He could not seem to find the right sound, and he quit recording completely for two years after its release. He knew he was ready for something different, but he was not quite sure what it would be. It was his respect for a few new emerging artists that helped him figure it out.

The Sound of Rock

By the mid-1960s, Davis was searching for a new type of music to play, and he found inspiration in several of the rock artists of the era, especially Jimi Hendrix and Sly Stone. He began spending a great deal of time with the two musicians. "We understood each other right away," Davis wrote about Hendrix. "He was a great blues guitarist. Both him and Sly were great natural musicians; they played what they heard."[1]

Davis's band began changing along with his music. As he relied more on electronic instruments to create a jazz/rock sound, some musicians left and new ones replaced them. Davis even hired a guitarist—a first for any of his bands. Some of those new players have become famous in the jazz world since then, including Herbie Hancock and Chick Corea. This new band, with the new funk sound, produced *In a Silent Way* and the still popular double album *Bitches Brew. Brew* hit the Top 40 and earned Davis his first gold record. The album even won a Grammy for best Large Group Jazz Performance.

During this period, Davis earned a nickname: the Prince of Darkness. How he got the nickname is not truly known. Certainly many of the jazz players of the time had nicknames—

Charlie Parker was Yardbird, John Birks Gillespie was Dizzy, and Louis Armstrong was Satchmo. Some thought it was because Davis was black; some thought it was due to the darkness of some of his music. Others, like Ian Carr, who wrote a definitive biography of Davis's life, say that the nickname was first used in 1967 when Davis released the album *Sorcerer*. One of the numbers on the album was called "Prince of Darkness," and sleeve notes, or comments written inside the album jacket, made a connection between Davis and the song.

A new series of tours was arranged for Davis and his band, and slowly these musicians created a style of music that blended the best of jazz and rock, often called fusion. This style brought Davis an all-new type of fan, but it did not necessarily please old jazz fans or the newspaper critics. Davis did not care one bit. He knew that his music would always please some people, and if they could not keep up with his changes—or chose not to—he felt it was their loss and never his.

Hard to Love
There was no question that Davis the musician had many fans. His albums were selling thousands of copies, his concerts were sold out, and he was being interviewed for all kinds of magazines and newspapers. Although countless fans had no trouble loving his music, it was often harder for them to like the man himself. After years of dealing with racial discrimination, and with a tendency toward shyness, Davis was not always kind to the people who loved him the most. During concerts, he would often turn his back to the audience while he played. He rarely ever spoke to the crowds and was often quite rude or vulgar to any fan or reporter who dared to approach him offstage.

Davis's frequent dark moods only got worse after a car accident in 1972 broke both of his ankles. Over the next few years, he received two hip replacements and a second operation on his throat. He was also treated for a bleeding ulcer. Finally, in 1975, he had had enough of the music world. He announced that he was retiring—and then he disappeared from the stage and recording studio. Was Miles Davis really finished with music?

Musical
Inspirations

Just as Miles Davis has inspired other musicians, Jimi Hendrix and Sly Stone were two musicians who inspired Davis. Hendrix was a rock guitarist who shared some of the same life challenges that Davis did. He lived with a series of different people as he grew up, and rarely saw his parents. After watching Elvis Presley perform, the teen saved up for his own guitar. He taught himself how to play and joined a band. After serving in the army as a paratrooper, he returned to music. In England, he met some of the most popular British musicians, including members of the Beatles, the Rolling Stones, and the Who.

Hendrix's first hit was "Hey Joe" in 1967, followed by "Purple Haze" and "The Wind Cried Mary." The world was in awe when he played "The Star-Spangled Banner" at the legendary Woodstock festival in 1969. Tragically, less than a year after this heartfelt performance, Hendrix died from drug-related problems. "The ultimate guitar player"[2] was only twenty-seven years old.

Unlike the other two musicians, Sly Stone (Sylvester Stewart) had a fairly stable childhood, singing in a family gospel group and working as a radio disc jockey. In the mid-1960s, Sly, along with his sister, brother, cousin, and three other musicians, formed the group Sly and the Family Stone. Their first album came out in 1967. Then, with hits like "Dance to the Music," "Everyday People," and "I Want to Take You Higher," they, too, were invited to play at Woodstock. The group continued to release albums through the mid-1970s, merging a strong beat, passionate guitar playing, and lyrics about tolerance and peace.

Jimi Hendrix

Chapter **5**

Making a Comeback

The mid-1970s were a dark and difficult time for Davis. He spent much of it inside his house with the curtains drawn, the doors locked, and the lights off. He was in physical pain from his car accident and from years of alcohol and drug abuse. In March 1976, *Rolling Stone* magazine reported rumors that this forty-nine-year-old musician was dying. In his autobiography, Davis recalled: "From 1975 until early 1980, I didn't pick up my horn; for over four years, didn't pick it up once. I would walk by and look at it, then think about trying to play. But after a while I didn't even do that."[1]

He admitted he was tired, in pain, and unhappy. "I became a hermit, hardly ever going outside," he wrote.[2] He had returned to using cocaine, and his life was falling apart around him. However, he had faith in his ability to recover. "I knew I could pick up my horn again whenever I wanted to," he wrote, "because my horn is as much a part of me as my eyes and hands."[3]

Back into the Studio

When Davis finally had had enough of retirement and came back to the recording studio, he did it alone. He no longer had his usual band with him, and at first, it was hard to master playing the trumpet the way he had before. He had not used his "chops," as he called his jaws

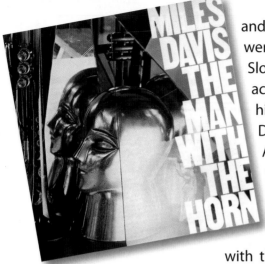

and lips, for several years. Those first songs were rough and most were never released. Slowly, he gathered new musicians to accompany him, and in 1981, he released his new album, *The Man with the Horn*. Davis began to feel alive and renewed. As he wrote in his life story, "When I was retired, I wasn't hearing any melodies in my head because I wouldn't let myself think about the music. But after being in the studio with those guys, I started hearing melodies again, and that made me feel good."[4] That same year, Davis married longtime on-and-off girlfriend Cicely Tyson.

Tyson, an actor and model, was born in 1933. She saw a different side of Miles Davis than his fans usually saw. She often spoke of him with great love. In an interview with *Ebony* magazine in 1981, she stated, "He's a beautiful human being. Really beautiful. That image, that reputation that he has is just a cover; it's a façade to protect the gentle being that's there."[5]

In early 1982, Davis suffered a stroke that temporarily left him unable to use his right arm. To help pass the time while he recovered, he began to paint. He would frequently spend five hours a day working on a painting. The hobby calmed him, and some of the art was used on his album covers. Some was even displayed in galleries throughout the United States, Japan, Spain, and Germany.

It was clear that music and painting were connected in his mind. He explained his painting process to trombonist Mike Zwerin in the *International Herald Tribune*. "The color. I get the color first. Then all the rest I improvise," he stated. "It's a matter of balance. You can't have too much black, black is heavy. Like you can't have too much saxophone."[6]

Despite his health, Davis was clearly on the road to a major comeback. He performed all over the world to sell-out crowds. Now and then, he was forced to take time off to take care of himself.

Cicely Tyson married Davis on November 26, 1981, and they stayed married until 1988. She starred in a number of television shows and films, including *Sounder, Roots, The Autobiography of Miss Jane Pittman,* and *Because of Winn-Dixie.*

Although Tyson had largely helped Davis get off drugs, he was still struggling with pain from his hip replacements and a bout of pneumonia. In 1985, he released *You're Under Arrest.*

The man who many had thought was permanently finished with making music was back, and he still had a few tricks up his sleeve.

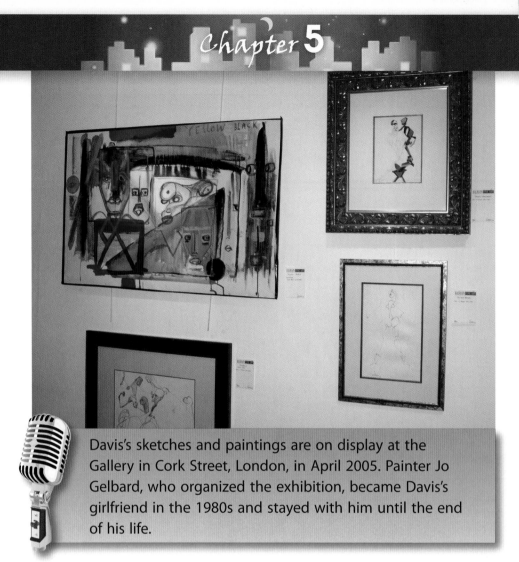

Davis's sketches and paintings are on display at the Gallery in Cork Street, London, in April 2005. Painter Jo Gelbard, who organized the exhibition, became Davis's girlfriend in the 1980s and stayed with him until the end of his life.

Davis had plans for new sounds and a new look. He had changed recording companies, leaving Columbia Records to join Warner Brothers. What would this amazing musician do next to surprise his fans?

Becoming a Legend

After decades of performing, improving, experimenting, changing, and recording dozens of hit albums, Miles Davis truly had become a legend in the jazz world. But calling him that never made him happy. He thought the term made him sound old and dull, rather than new and exciting—the way he wanted his music to be.

Davis had a distinct sound when he played, largely because he thought he played the way he spoke. In an interview with *Jazz*

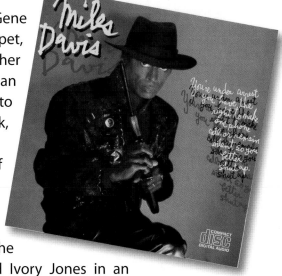

Magazine, he told reporter Gene Kalbacher, "It's my tone on the trumpet, it sounds like I'm speakin'. In other words, an instrument should be an extension of you; it's supposed to sound like you—the way you walk, the way you dress, you know."[7]

Keeping with his tradition of always changing his image and his approach to music, Davis appeared on television in 1986. First, he showed up as a character on the police series *Miami Vice*. He played Ivory Jones in an episode called "Junk Love." Later, he made a number of short Honda Scooter commercials, as well as radio commercials for a jazz station. The fame those advertisements brought him made Davis a little angry. "After you make all this music, please all these people with your playing, and are known all over the world, you find out that all it takes is one commercial to put you over the top in people's minds," he wrote.[8]

That same year, he was awarded an honorary Doctorate of Music from the New England Conservatory of Music to honor his lifetime of musical achievements. In 1990, he was given a Grammy for those same accomplishments. He published his autobiography, *Miles,* and it became a bestseller. Near the end of it, he wrote, "For me, the urgency to play and create music today is worse than when I started. It's more intense. It's like a curse." He added that he went to bed thinking about music and woke up still thinking about it. For that, he was grateful, writing, "I love that it hasn't abandoned me; I feel really blessed."[9] Of course, Davis continued to record and release albums, including *Tutu* in 1986, and *Music from Siesta* in 1987.

Going Back to the Originals
As the 1980s passed and a new decade started, Davis's performances started taking an unexpected turn. After playing a new style of music

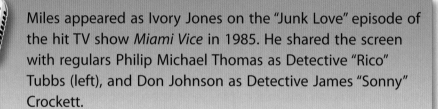

Miles appeared as Ivory Jones on the "Junk Love" episode of the hit TV show *Miami Vice* in 1985. He shared the screen with regulars Philip Michael Thomas as Detective "Rico" Tubbs (left), and Don Johnson as Detective James "Sonny" Crockett.

known as doo-bop with rapper Easy Mo Bee, Davis began to perform some of his classics on stage. He did old favorites that people had not heard him play in years. He appeared all over the world, from the Hollywood Bowl in Los Angeles to the jazz festival in Montreux, Switzerland. He played at the Amnesty International Concert at Giants Stadium in New Jersey as well. Old fans were thrilled and the critics were pleased, but others were confused. Why this return to the past?

Some people wondered if somehow Davis knew that his time was running short and he wanted to give his audiences what they

loved the most before he was gone. He had already been diagnosed with a range of ailments, from diabetes and sickle cell anemia to bleeding ulcers and throat polyps. In September 1991, Davis was taken to Saint John's Health Center in Santa Monica, California. He had a severe case of bronchial pneumonia, a problem that had plagued him in the past. While he was being treated, he experienced a second stroke, and soon he was in a coma. Davis died on September 28, at the age of sixty-five. He left behind three sons, one daughter, and seven grandchildren.

Davis also left behind endless stories, amazing music, vibrant paintings, and continual inspiration to trumpeters and other jazz musicians. His passion for music and his talent on the trumpet helped inspire and encourage many of these people. His songs live in these new performers as they struggle to become as skilled as he was when

One of Davis's last public performances was on November 3, 1990. He played alongside bass player Foley McCreary at the Zenith in Paris.

Davis's family accepted his induction into the Rock and Roll Hall of Fame. From left to right are his daughter Cheryl, nephew Vincent Wilburn Jr., son Gregory, grandson Paul Scott, and youngest son Erin.

he played the tunes. Some of the dozens of people he jammed with became famous on their own. Besides Chick Corea and Herbie Hancock, these include John Coltrane, Branford Marsalis, and Kenny Garrett. In this way, Davis's dedication and skills will never be lost but carried on from one generation of musicians to the next. In fact, his son Erin Davis and nephew Vince Wilburn Jr. are helping to continue his legacy. In 2008, they produced the album *Miles from India,* which was a cross-cultural collaboration that celebrated the music of Miles Davis. Musicians who had played with Miles and new musicians from India came together to create this album.[10] Erin and Vince continue to manage his estate, promoting the man and his music. By 2012, two movies about Miles Davis were in the works.

Miles Davis may have preferred the nickname Prince of Darkness, but for most of the world, he truly was a legendary jazz master.

An Artist's Art

Music was not the only kind of art that Davis produced. He also sketched and painted. "My father taught me when we were real small," he recalled. "He had all of us drawing, because St. Louis was a prejudiced place and it took the edge off of things. It takes a lot of anger out." He added, "If you're gonna get mad, and you sit down and sketch a bit, it will leave."[11]

His drawings were used on the covers and liners of several of his albums, and his artwork has been displayed throughout the United States and even in Europe. "If I draw something, it's what I want to see right then," Davis told writer Ken Franckling in a 1986 interview. "When I go to a hotel, if the room is full, I have my colors. I take a piece of paper, and the room changes. You know what I mean?"[12]

Davis's paintings cover a wide range of styles and subjects. Art gallery owner Gary Lajeski once compared Davis's art to music. "They're really kind of quick study sketches with a lot of humor in them," he said, "[like] musical notes flowing across the page."[13] Davis often said that he had been inspired by the art of Pablo Picasso. Some of the designs were brightly colored sketches of jazz players on stage *(Jazz)*, while others, like *Roots*, explore the musician's fascination with his African-American heritage. Davis's artwork continues to be displayed, and copies of it are sold on the Internet.

Miles Davis painting, *Twilight Magic*

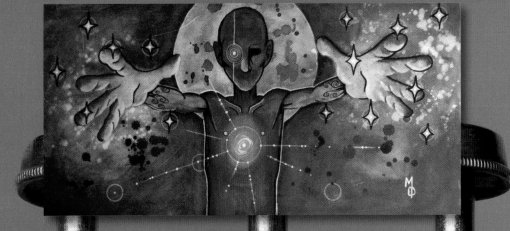

1926   Miles Dewey Davis III is born on May 25 in Alton, Illinois.

1935   He is given his first trumpet.

1939   He receives a nicer trumpet for his birthday, which includes lessons with Elwood Buchanan.

1940   He begins playing with local bands.

1944   He graduates from high school and begins his studies at Juilliard School of Music. His parents divorce. His daughter, Cheryl, is born.

1945   Davis drops out of Juilliard to play full-time with bands.

1946   His son, Gregory, is born.

1949–

  1950   The Miles Davis Nonet records *Birth of the Cool.*

1950   His son Miles Dewey Davis IV is born.

1953   Davis goes to his father's estate to kick a drug addiction.

1954   He kicks his addiction for good in a Detroit, Michigan, hotel room.

1955   He performs at the Newport Jazz Festival in Rhode Island. Columbia Records gives him a contract.

1957   He has surgery to remove polyps on his throat.

1958   He marries Frances Taylor.

1959   *Kind of Blue,* which becomes the highest-selling jazz album in history, is released. He is beaten by a New York City police officer when he refuses to "move along."

1961   Davis becomes the highest-paid jazz player in the country.

1968   His divorce from Taylor becomes final. He marries aspiring soul singer Betty Mabry; the marriage lasts a year, but they do not divorce for three years.

1970   He releases *Bitches Brew,* which hits the Top 40 and earns a gold record and a Grammy Award. His son Erin is born.

1972   He is involved in a serious car accident that breaks both his ankles.

1975   He has surgery for hip replacement and ulcers; he retires at the end of the year.

1981   He returns to performing; releases *The Man with the Horn;* and marries actress Cicely Tyson.

1982   Davis has his first stroke. He begins to paint.

1986   He is given an honorary Doctorate of Music from New England Conservatory; appears on television shows and commercials; performs old classics in multiple concerts.

1988   He and Tyson divorce.

1991   The Australian movie *Dingo,* in which he plays the part of jazz trumpeter Billy Cross and for which he wrote the sound track, is released. He begins recording new songs in doo-bop style with rapper Easy Mo Bee. Davis dies on September 28 at Saint John's Health Center in Santa Monica, California.

2008   Erin Davis and his cousin, Vince Wilburn Jr., produce and market the album *Miles from India*.

2012   The U.S. Postal Service issues a stamp featuring Edith Piaf and Miles Davis. Two movies about the life of Miles Davis are in production.

Discography

1945   *Miles Davis/Savoy Jazz*

1946   *Bopping the Blues/Black Lion*

1947   *Miles Davis/Joker*

1948   *Miles Davis and His Tuba Band: Pre-birth of the Cool*

1949   *The Miles Davis/Tadd Dameron Quintet in Paris Festival International de Jazz*

1950   *Miles Davis "At Birdland"*

1951   *Sonny Rollins: First Recordings*

1952   *Miles Davis/Jimmy Forrest: Live at the Barrel, Volume One and Volume Two*

Miles Davis/Volume 1

1953   *Early Miles/Prestige; Miles Davis and the Lighthouse All-Stars: At Last!*

1954   *Miles Davis/Volume 2/Blue Note; Miles Davis: Walkin'; Miles Davis and the Modern Jazz Giants*

1955   *Miles Davis: Blue Moods; Odyssey*

1956   *Miles Davis: Oleo; Miles Davis: Steamin'; Miles Davis: Relaxin'; Music for Brass; Miles Davis: Cookin'*

1957   *Miles Davis + 19: Miles Ahead; Ascenseur pour l'echafaud; The Complete Amsterdam Concert*

1958   *Milestones; 1958 Miles; Cannonball Adderley: Somethin' Else; At Newport 1958; Porgy and Bess; Jazz at the Plaza, Vol. 1*

1959   *Miles Davis and John Coltrane: Live in New York; Kind of Blue; Sketches of Spain*

1960   *Miles Davis and John Coltrane: Live in Stockholm 1960; The Miles Davis Quintet Live in Zurich 1960; Free Trade Hall Vol.1; Free Trade Hall Vol. 2; Miles Davis and Sonny Stitt: Live in Stockholm 1960*

1961   *Someday My Prince Will Come; Miles Davis in Person: Friday Night at the Blackhawk, San Francisco, Vol.1 and Vol. II; Miles Davis at Carnegie Hall; Live Miles*

1963   *Quiet Nights; Seven Steps to Heaven; Live at Newport 1963; Miles Davis Quintet: Cote Blues*

1964   *Miles in Tokyo; Miles in Berlin; Miles Davis—Paris, France; The Complete Copenhagen Concert 1964*

1965   *E.S.P.; Live at the Plugged Nickel*

Chapter Notes

Chapter 1. Weathering an Argument

1. Miles Davis with Quincey Troupe, *Miles: The Autobiography* (New York: Simon and Schuster, 1989), p. 28.
2. Ibid., p. 29.
3. Ibid., p. 31.
4. Ibid., p. 40.
5. Ibid., p. 30.

Chapter 2. Getting an Early Start

1. Miles Davis with Quincey Troupe, *Miles: The Autobiography* (New York: Simon and Schuster, 1989), p. 18.
2. Ian Carr, *Miles Davis, the Definitive Biography* (New York: Thunder's Mouth Press, 1998), p. 13.
3. Bill Kirchner, *A Miles Davis Reader* (Smithsonian Institution Press: Washington, 1997), p. 6.
4. Davis, p. 74.
5. Ibid.

Chapter 3. Breaking an Addiction

1. Miles Davis with Quincey Troupe, *Miles: The Autobiography* (New York: Simon and Schuster, 1989), p. 136.
2. Ibid., pp. 169–170.
3. Ibid., p. 170.
4. Ibid., p. 174.

Chapter 4. Hitting the Charts—and Getting Hit

1. Miles Davis with Quincey Troupe, *Miles: The Autobiography* (New York: Simon and Schuster, 1989), p. 293.
2. A&E Television Networks: Jimi Hendrix Biography, http://www.biography.com/people/jimi-hendrix-9334756

Chapter 5. Making a Comeback

1. Miles Davis with Quincey Troupe, *Miles: The Autobiography* (New York: Simon and Schuster, 1989), p. 333.
2. Ibid., p. 335.
3. Ibid., p. 341.
4. Ibid., p. 344.
5. "Cicely Tyson," *Ebony,* February 1981.
6. Ian Carr, *Miles Davis, the Definitive Biography* (New York: Thunder's Mouth Press, 1998), p. 491.
7. Gene Kalbacher, *Jazz Magazine,* April 3, 1985.
8. Davis and Troupe, p. 376.
9. Ibid., pp. 411–412.
10. Jazz Monthly.com. "Jazz Monthly Feature Interview: Miles Davis—A Son's Perspective (Erin Davis; also Nephew Vince Wilburn Jr.") *Jazz Monthly,* June 2008. http://www.jazzmonthly.com/artist_ag/davis_miles/interviews/miles_davis_index.html
11. Ken Franckling, "The Prince of Darkness Turns 60: 'I Know What I've Done for Music, but Don't Call Me "A Legend," ' " Jazz Journalists Association Library, May 18, 1986, http://www.jazzhouse.org/library/?read=franckling1
12. Ibid.
13. Ibid.

BOOKS

Crease, Stephanie Stein. *Duke Ellington: His Life in Jazz with 21 Activities.* Chicago: Chicago Review Press, 2009.

Dell, Pamela. *Miles Davis: Jazz Master.* Chanhassen, MN: The Child's World, 2005.

Lynette, Rachel. *Miles Davis: Legendary Jazz Musician.* Farmington Hills, MI: KidHaven Press, 2010.

WORKS CONSULTED

All About Jazz; Miles Davis Discography.
http://www.allaboutjazz.com/php/musician_discography.php?id=6144

Carner, Gary. *The Miles Davis Companion: Four Decades of Commentary.* Omnibus Press: New York, 1996.

Carr, Ian. *Miles Davis: The Definitive Biography.* New York: Thunder's Mouth Press, 1998.

Chambers, J.K. *Milestones: The Music and Times of Miles Davis.* New York: Da Capo Press, 1998.

Davis, Gregory, with Les Sussman. *Dark Magus: The Jekyll and Hide Life of Miles Davis.* San Francisco: Backbeat Books, 2006.

Davis, Miles, with Quincy Troupe. *Miles: The Autobiography.* New York: Simon and Schuster, 1989.

"Ebony Interview: Cicely Tyson." *Ebony,* February 1981, pp. 121–132.

Franckling, Ken. "The Prince of Darkness Turns 60: 'I know What I've Done for Music, but Don't Call Me "a Legend." ' " Jazz Journalists Association Library, May 18, 1986, http://www.jazzhouse.org/library/?read=franckling1

Jazz Monthly.com. "Jazz Monthly Feature Interview: Miles Davis—A Son's Perspective (Erin Davis; also Nephew Vince Wilburn Jr.)." *Jazz Monthly,* June 2008. http://www.jazzmonthly.com/artist_ag/davis_miles/interviews/miles_davis_index.html

Kalbacher, Gene. "I Think the Greatest Sound in the World is the Human Voice." *Jazz,* April 3, 1985, Issue 5. http://hepcat1950.com/mdiv8504.html

Kirchner, Bill, editor. *A Miles Davis Reader.* Washington, D.C.: Smithsonian Institution Press, 1997.

Maher, Paul, Jr. *Miles on Miles: Interviews and Encounters with Miles Davis.* Chicago: Lawrence Hill Books, 2009.

Pareles, Jon. "Miles Davis, Trumpeter, Dies: Jazz Genius, 65, Defined Cool." *The New York Times,* September 29, 1991. http://www.nytimes. com/1991/09/29/nyregion/miles-davis-trumpeter-dies-jazz-genius-65-defined-cool.html?pagewanted=1

ON THE INTERNET

The Biography Channel, "Miles Davis Biography"
 http://www.thebiographychannel.co.uk/biographies/miles-davis.html
Jazz Biographies: "Miles Davis"
 http://www.pbs.org/jazz/biography/artist_id_davis_miles.htm
Miles Davis Online
 http://www.milesdavisonline.com/
PBS Kids: Jazz Greats, "Miles Davis"
 http://pbskids.org/jazz/nowthen/miles.html

bebop—A style of jazz that was known for complex harmony and rhythms.

cornet (kor-NET)—A brass instrument similar to but smaller than a trumpet.

funk—A style of jazz that was known for blending soul and blues and containing a strong rhythm for dancing.

fusion (FYOO-jhun)—A kind of popular music that is a blend of two or more styles, such as jazz and funk.

heroin (HAYR-oh-in)—A strong, dangerous, and highly addictive drug.

jazz (JAZ)—A type of music that developed from the blues to have a strong, lively beat and for which players often make up musical phrases on the spot.

jukebox (JOOK-boks)—A coin-operated machine that plays music selected by the customer.

nonet (noh-NET)—A combination of nine instruments and voices; the music written for a group of nine.

polyp (PAH-lip)—A growth on a mucus-producing part of the body.

prejudice (PREH-joo-diss)—Hostile attitude against a particular group.

quartet (kwar-TET)—A group of four.

quintet (kwin-TET)—A combination of five instruments and voices; the music written for a group of nine.

sextet (sex-TET)—A combination of six instruments and voices.

solo (SOH-loh)—A performance done by only one person.

ulcer (UL-ser)—A sore on the skin or on an internal part of the body.

About the Author

Tamra Orr is the author of more than 250 nonfiction books for readers of all ages, including biographies of celebrities and sports stars. She graduated from Ball State University in Muncie, Indiana. She lives in the Pacific Northwest with her family. Her husband is a jazz fan and introduced her to the sounds of Miles Davis—one of the many things she thanks him for. *Sketches of Spain* was the perfect background music as she wrote this book.